Wedding Traditions
from
Around the World
COLORING BOOK

Brenda Sneathen Mattox

DOVER PUBLICATIONS, INC.
Mineola, New York

Publisher's Note

Wedding traditions, while changing considerably over the years, enable cultural groups to maintain their ties with the past through rituals and customs. For instance, in the medieval era, courtship—or even meeting one's prospective spouse—was sometimes not an option. Instead, men kidnapped their chosen brides from other tribes or clans. That practice established certain customs. To help seize his bride, for instance, the groom summoned fellow warriors, whom we now call the best man and groomsmen. According to some historians, the "honeymoon" followed: for the next month, or moon, the groom hid his new bride from her angry family, who anxiously searched for her.

Later, when brides were permitted to choose their husbands, further traditions developed in world cultures, particularly regarding the supernatural. A bride wore a veil as a disguise, to confuse harmful spirits. Bridesmaids dressed identically to the bride, as decoys, to fool the evil eye. To ward off demons, the first wedding bouquets were made of pungent herbs, garlic and thyme. Other wedding traditions were rooted in practicality. The wedding kiss originally meant not eternal love, but the acceptance of a legal contract. And today's towering, extravagantly decorated wedding cake evolved from humble grains of wheat, or chunks of bread, thrown at the bride to encourage fertility.

Today's brides and grooms often choose to honor their ethnic or cultural heritage with a special tradition. Here is a fascinating collection of 29 depictions of authentic and dramatic wedding customs, just waiting for your touch of color!

Bibliographical Note

Wedding Traditions from Around the World is a new work, first published by Dover Publications, Inc., in 2007.

International Standard Book Number
ISBN-13: 978-486-46232-5
ISBN-10: 0-486-46232-3

Manufactured in the United States of America
Dover Publications, Inc., 31 East 2nd Street, Mineola, N.Y. 11501

African wedding traditions are as diverse as the continent's many cultures. However, the "tying of the knot" custom occurs quite frequently. Here, a strip of leather binds the hands of a Nigerian couple in their traditional *buba*s (blouses).

To insure a happy marriage, the **Austrian** bride's gown should stay unfinished until she leaves for church. Here, a bridesmaid takes a final stitch at the last moment. And believe it or not, it's lucky for a bride to see a *black* cat!

A **Balinese** wedding dazzles the eye! Both the bride and groom wear *songket*, a beautiful golden fabric, as well as jewelry and headdresses. At the close of the elaborate ceremony, the couple is declared married as a flower is tied to each forehead with a ribbon.

5

Red is *the* color for a **Chinese** wedding! The bride's gown, invitations, even gift boxes are red, to signify love, joy, and good fortune. Here, the couple at the altar pays homage to the heavens, the earth, and their ancestors. They then bow to one another, becoming

husband and wife. Sometimes the groom removes a knotted sash from his chest and gives one end to his bride before they bow. The Chinese characters in the picture mean "double happiness."

The ribbon pull is a lovely **English** Victorian ritual for bridesmaids. When the wedding cake is assembled, beribboned charms, each with a special significance, are placed between the layers. Before the bride and groom cut the cake, each bridesmaid pulls a ribbon for her charm.

This **Finnish** couple and their guests have eaten a lavish pre-wedding breakfast. Now the wedding party forms a lively procession to the church, accompanied by fiddlers. The bride's elaborate headdress and collar are made of colorful ribbons.

The *globe de mariée,* or wedding globe, was a popular nineteenth-century tradition in **France**. In this example from Brittany, the dove with laurel wreath signifies peace and harmony, the roses and daisies signify love, the diamond-shaped mirrors signify fertility, the oak leaves signify longevity, and the shamrocks signify luck.

10

One noisy, messy **German** wedding tradition is the *polterabend*. Guests bring plates and bowls and break them on the ground, and the couple then sweeps up the pieces. According to German lore, "*Scherben bringen Gluck!*" (Broken crockery brings you luck!).

The **Greek** wedding ceremony concludes with the *koumbaros*, the best man or groom's godfather, placing joined wreaths of orange blossoms on the couple's heads. The wheat sheaves on the candles represent fertility.

The **Hawaiian** bride wears a *holoku,* a white, formal muumuu. The groom wears a white shirt and pants with a red sash. Both have *haku* wreaths, and he also wears two leis, one of orange *ilima* flowers and another of *maile* leaves. His bride's lei is made of white *pikake,* fragrant white jasmine.

13

Indian weddings are lavish and colorful affairs, often lasting for days. Of the many Indian marriage customs, one of the most important is shown here. For *Rajaham,* Sacrifice to the Sacred Fire, the bride and groom symbolically purify their hands with the fire, then throw in a handful of rice.

The Claddagh ring is popular among **Irish** couples. On it, the hands represent faith, the crown honor, and the heart, love. Traditionally, an engaged woman wears it on the right hand, and a married woman wears the ring on her left hand. In double-ring ceremonies, many grooms choose Claddagh rings as wedding bands.

Dancing is an important part of **Italian** wedding receptions, from the *tarantella*, a lively circle dance, to waltzes and contemporary dances. Any man wishing to dance with the bride must pay her cash, which she tucks into her satin bag, called *la borsa*.

A **Japanese** couple performs a wedding ritual called *sansan-kudo*, sharing nine sips of sake (rice wine). Here they are shown using a mallet to open the keg. Many couples serve lobster at the reception, because its red color is thought to bring good luck.

The **Jewish** bridal ceremony is traditionally performed under a canopy called a *chuppah*. At the conclusion, the groom, wearing his *talit* or prayer scarf, steps on a wrapped glass, breaking it. Then the guests all shout *"Mazel tov!"* to wish the couple good fortune.

In some Asian cultures, the wedding reception is almost more important than the ceremony itself. In **Korea**, the party is called *Kook Soo Sang,* or "Noodle Banquet," because noodles represent happiness and long life. Nuts, jujubes and dates, symbolizing a fruitful union, are also part of the feast. Here, the bridal couple shares a date.

A wedding celebration in **Morocco** can last as long as a week! The bride is treated like a queen and dressed like one too. After the simple wedding rite, she is carried into the reception on a litter by her *negaffa* (bridesmaids).

Among the different **Native American** peoples, many observe this tradition: The groom shares his blanket with his bride, they circle a fire three times, and then drink water from a special two-spouted wedding goblet.

The traditional **Norwegian** bride wears an elaborate headdress decorated with silver bangles. As she moves, they tinkle, a sound thought to ward off evil spirits. She or her bridesmaids sometimes favor green for their gowns, a color other cultures may consider unlucky.

In the **Philippines**, the best man takes the bride's veil and pins it to the groom's shoulder, symbolizing that they are clothed as one. Then the maid of honor places a knotted white cord around the couple to represent their bond.

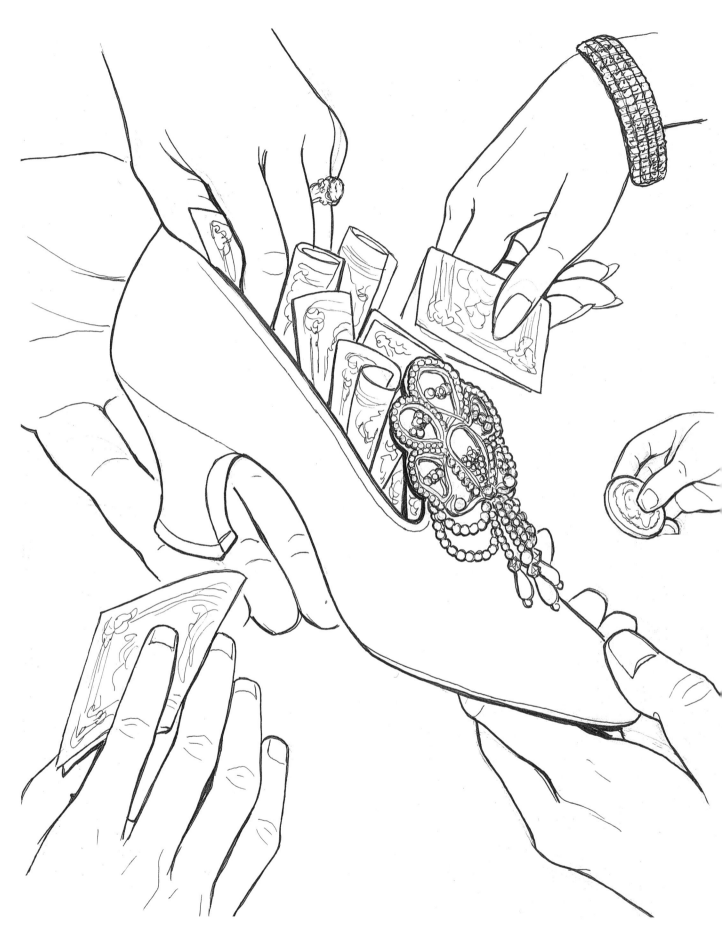

After the wedding ceremony, **Portuguese** guests throw candy and flowers, instead of rice, at the newlyweds. At the reception, the bride's shoe is passed among the guests to hold gifts of money.

According to ancient Celtic lore, evil spirits who lurk beneath the threshold might seize a new bride or cause her to stumble. That's why the canny **Scots** groom carries her inside! Her tartan scarf indicates that she has joined her husband's clan.

Most **South American** countries share the ritual of the *arras*. Here, the groom presents his bride with thirteen gold coins, representing Christ and the twelve apostles, blessed by the priest. Thus, the groom symbolically endows the bride with all his worldly goods.

Many cultures incorporate orange blossoms into weddings, but almost surely the tradition originated in **Spain.** Because the orange tree flowers and fruits at the same time, it represents both purity and fertility for the bride.

In **Thailand,** the mothers place joined flower garlands on the bride's and groom's heads. At the conclusion of the wedding ceremony, the eldest relative, for good luck, washes the hands of the couple with water from a conch shell.

In **Tibet**, every guest gives the couple a *hada*, a white scarf that represents blessings. Sometimes the bride and groom are nearly buried in *hadas!* In this picture, the couple shares some barley beer.

Brides and grooms in the **United States** cut the cake, then feed each other a small piece, a ritual often pictured in the wedding album. This custom symbolizes the couple's vow to nourish and nurture one another.

In **West Java**, among the **Sundanese**, the bride and groom participate in the *Nincak Endog,* or egg-breaking ritual. He breaks an egg with his foot, symbolizing he will be master of the house. To show that she will serve him, the bride then washes his foot with water from the *kendi* jug, a symbol of peace. She seals her promise by breaking the jug.

In the **Western United States**, the bride and groom sometimes wear traditional cowboy hats and boots. The horseshoe hanging above them, an ancient symbol of good fortune, is positioned in a "U." According to legend, that keeps the good luck from spilling out!